The National Poetry Seri the publication of five colle....... ..., ,... ... participating publishers. *The Series is funded annually by Amazon Literary Partnership, the Gettinger Family Foundation, Bruce Gibney, HarperCollins Publishers, The Stephen and Tabitha King Foundation, Lannan Foundation, Newman's Own Foundation, Anna and Olafur Olafsson, Penguin Random House, the Poetry Foundation, Elise and Steven Trulaske, and the National Poetry Series Board of Directors.*

THE NATIONAL POETRY SERIES WINNERS
OF 2019 OPEN COMPETITION

Field Music by Alexandria Hall
Chosen by Rosanna Warren for Ecco

Little Big Bully by Heid Erdrich
Chosen by Amy Gerstler for Penguin Books

Fractal Shores by Diane Louie
Chosen by Sherod Santos for University of Georgia Press

Thrown in the Throat by Benjamin Garcia
Chosen by Kazim Ali for Milkweed Editions

An Incomplete List of Names by Michael Torres
Chosen by Raquel Salas Rivera for Beacon Press

Fractal Shores

Fractal Shores

Poems

Diane Louie

THE UNIVERSITY OF GEORGIA PRESS

ATHENS

© 2020 by the University of Georgia Press

Athens, Georgia 30602

www.ugapress.org

All rights reserved

Set in 11/17 Palatino

Printed and bound by Sheridan Books, Inc.

The paper in this book meets the guidelines for permanence and durability of the Committee on Production Guidelines for Book Longevity of the Council on Library Resources.

Most University of Georgia Press titles are available from popular e-book vendors.

Printed in the United States of America

20 21 22 23 24 P 5 4 3 2 1

Library of Congress Control Number: 2020943251

ISBN: 9780820357904 (pbk.: alk. paper)

ISBN: 9780820357911 (ebook)

CONTENTS

Fractal Shores

BLUEBIRD

Where it isn't is what we talk about. The Navajo rug between us holds a history of the world: birds sheltered in the leaves of a cornstalk. The woman weaving was expecting a child. The bluebird was then left out. Had we not been told we would not have known to wonder. That is the history of a moment. This another: one winter one hundred bluebirds descended to the branches of an oak tree beside the house where I grew up. My mother says they were on the other side, in ivy overhanging garbage cans my father had enclosed in wood to keep raccoons from prying off the lids. All that sudden blue alighting, lifting up, alighting in those bare black winter branches. History, shared, sheds time for the trace between. That moment, like blue in the stun of winter, in the distance of sky, in the nanostructure of feather barbs, was never really there. Like a child, it left what's missing.

On Balance:
Denis Josselin Crossing the Seine

If we are what we leave behind, *then* what is the sky with its shifting horizons? The river bisecting land. The ligature of windblown trees. Even in a raspberry silk blouson, a man is but the wind's apostrophe. So far as I can see from the deck of a white péniche. I am looking up, with apéritif, and wonder. Such a spectacle of trust, each step he takes. Above the river. Below the sky. Such concatenation, each one by one. Through my binoculars he smiles. His gray hair curls. The silk blouson is not tucked in. One must be authorized to cross above the Seine: the high steel wire made familiar, the weighted black pole. He is not walking on air. Nor am I, and yet it is my birthday. I am crossing from *you-must-be-kidding* to *what-if-what-if.* He kneels. I hold my breath. He stretches out. He wraps a scarf across his eyes. *If* shifting *now* and *then.*

De Sequana VSLM

My gift is modest: a fleck of mica. *Votem solvit libens merito.* One brings to Sequana that which needs to be healed. This will not be uncovered on an archeological dig. Nor will it be stolen. *So-and-so gives you her vow.* And yet I myself pried loose the black-edged flake from its granite boulder, the boulder last transported by Quaternary ice, that vast glacier equally allochthonous. As I become, in coming here. Matted leaves, sphagnum moss, wicks of knotted grass. And a tiny slip of mica: for seeing-through. For egress and reflection. *Bassin Sacré.* A ribbon-shimmer surfacing becomes the Seine. Sequana's open-handed welcome gives to journey meaning. First the day, then the world to come.

VISITING GERTRUDE STEIN IN PÈRE-LACHAISE

which is real what you do now or what you used to do

Her stone is not the largest. Polished gray, edges square. Her name engraved. One could stand on it. One could sit. Others have placed stones upon the stone. Gravity would do as well. Bones don't expatriate from earth. But a name. Among so many names. Every heart once beating on its own. Trees weep. Seeds scatter to the gravel path, perfect seeds. Imperfect seeds. The wars we have seen. The sky is so convincing, but wars? Each replaced by the one which follows. You never think it's going to be like this. You never think the thinking ends. I am sitting on a wooden bench. For the view, for the vale between. I have walked to her door. I have walked away. Atoms, all atoms. All quivering space.

FLYING COLORS

Ceci est la couleur de mes rêves.

JOAN MIRÓ, 1925

This is the color of my dreams, Miró tagged forget-me-not blue. Miró, faceless, has taken my hand. Before we named it, we did not see the sky. We still confuse each other with ourselves. The sky in our veins, our blood in the soil. Only from a distance does the Universe repeat itself: red blooming to red, blue basking in blue. On our side of heaven, mudslinging makes house calls, but Miró's still the gardener of empty space. Cerulean blue daub culled from two scallops of blue. How will we see in common if we don't take someone's part? Oh! Let us rise to the occasion of our one and only heart.

ONLY CONNECT

Above terra cotta roof tiles contrails crisscross the sky like math symbols mooring relation: *equal to, not equal to*: seeds of ice, spreading as thin white veils. One condensed against another, formed in the wake of thinking: *equal to not equal to*. As waves, fronts, ridges, troughs, earth's rotation moves our view around. A woman leans out her window to water blooming lavender. A green bird is perched behind the telephone. As wind, as direction and force: we make the bed we do not want to sleep in. How much thinking clouds our thinking: the body, conversing for the mind. We want to sing. We want to lift both hands to the sky. Ah, for a firmament of song! *Equal to not equal too*: the telephone has no battery, the bird is painted wood. The woman is made known by pen and ink. But we ourselves are saying so! Imagine that!

Even in Paris

Spring lags behind rain's liaison. No one minds, the mind fills in. There's always someone to sing it, in Paris, always someone with a song. A ladybug passed palm to palm, a *lady's bird*, a *little Messiah of Moses*. Propping up a loudspeaker in Église Saint-Louis, a pair of angels offer *dona nobis pacem* canted in flirtation. And yet, before he was a saint, Saint Louis burned twelve thousand sacred books of Jews. Siren, accordion, some songs are sorrow's afterthought. A woman sashays damp rags across the stone choir floor. Wet wings make verses of the air. Our silence, refrain.

SET IN MOTION

We are learning our father where our father stood. Late afternoon spills from the sun. Shells flock with shadows on the outgoing tide. I am skirting the subject. Everyone should have one, said my father. A crowbar. My father was poking through the rotting corner of our redwood deck. And a sledgehammer. We were still children in our father's eyes, seated on corkscrew wooden stools with newsprint and graphite pencils, drawing the contours of our father's head, his nose, his neck, the curve of his spine. My father was prying loose, then piling rusted nails. How hard they work, the six external muscles of the eye: up, down, left, right, rotate left and right. When Marie Tharp mapped the backbone of earth, first in fathoms, then in corrected fathoms, then in the metric system, one thing led to another, the continents moving closer, the oceans moving apart. There you are, said my father, you're set to go. We are planting *Helianthus* in the footprint of a redwood deck. There are no old rocks on the ocean floor. There is no surface to the sun.

The Mathematics of Over and Done With

doesn't add up

always something missing, your voice your still-with-us marking
time making tea mincing *dangs* to the squirrels on the feeder you fill
for the jays, a digit, a sneeze

        can't take away

step ladders, plexiglass, a gallery wall, words etched in seafoam
and silvery gray—floating, fluorescent-lit—*dear one, dear one, dearly
departed*

        times

u-turning on a Nevada county road for hundreds of shoes flung
over the branches of a cottonwood tree, frayed velcro, splayed
laces, a lone once-white brassiere

        and then divided

by the last trace of a growing edge curled in a spiral or stretched
to a cone—*good bye god be*—that small shell pocketed or left on the
road, it is one and the same

What Happened Was This

Stretched Pebble Canyon, Death Valley

We followed each other toward a wall of gray stone. Across a dry wash. Across coalescent alluvial fans. We walked on stones the hills once were, the sea the stone once was, the salt, the silt of shells. The sun was in our eyes. It was not yet spring. We walked through a rift in the wall. Without even a word. The crunch of sand, of crushed marble and schist, of eighteen hundred million years. We walked. We counted our steps. The walls closed in. Visible and vulnerable, the human body, ventured by nativity. Feathers would never be protection. Nor songs of Purcell sung aloud. We climbed. We threaded our way. Footholds, handholds, we scaled dry falls. The abacus of motion slowed, and slowed the morning lengthened. A swath of orange light tithed the high canyon wall. Above, a fluttered blue ribbon of sky. We stretched. We reached through the umbra for more than ourselves. Austerity gave us the word *silhouette*. Sunlight gave us a hand.

Isis Among Us

Je suis ce qui a été
ce qui est et ce qui sera
et nul mortel n'a encore levé
le voile qui me couvre.

INSCRIPTION ON STATUE OF ISIS, GODDESS OF LIFE,
HERBERT HOOVER NATIONAL HISTORIC SITE, WEST BRANCH, IOWA

In her stone robes, in the folds of her massive limbs, we wake like the moon which breaks itself to heal, unencumbered by earth's dark habits, fields haunted by listing silos, graves, just graves, the rust of tractors. We wake to find we've slept into our day's long shadow, reaching for a place we mean to reach, stunned by meaning we thought we'd left behind. But as the moon hammocked in the loam of stars returns to stars light drawn of the sun, so even words repatriate eventually to *love*, material of our earth on which this great stone keeper waits, her feet buried in our soil, her hands solid in our laps, her half-curved fœtal eyes pressing the weight of our own stone veil.

POSSIBLY, WE

Take that cat, Schrödinger, and the box he didn't die in, and the jonquils growing round the grave, and the path we could have made deciphering the bones, and the silence we have kept instead, and the cat we never named, and the box we haven't closed, and the long walk we've had to walk to get away. Take what the wind takes indiscriminately—stones and souls and soughing pines—take the bonbon box of bullets, take these sighs, take us, take that night's kiss that found us kissing and the light we didn't light, and our trouble and our truth, take what interferes with sight. For all we've waved, for all we've hammered at that box, even Schrödinger must see what we've left is what we've come to be.

Taking into Consideration

> *Astronomers are continuing their frequent observations of Io, providing a long-term database of high spatial resolution images that not even Galileo, which orbited Jupiter for eight years, was able to achieve.*
>
> BERKELEY NEWS

Io is my sister. I know her distance, I share her beveled voice. She never asked for Jupiter's attention. Nor I for the bollocks of Italy. The rain she ran through, trees she ducked, thorns, snapped branches snafued on fences. The truth she traced in dirt. By the time Galileo glimpsed her, she would only emerge at night. It takes more than *per aspera ad astra* to protest against the universe. Galileo called her *Cosmica Sideris* to make good with the family Medici. We call her a Galilean moon in point of NASA's exploration. But Io was my sister first. Italy, a cloud.

In Our Country

When spring comes we know it by the pale pink waxy stems of Indian pipe, *M. uniflora* unfurling in shade, green wands of narcissus, *N. pseudonarcissus* in the last patches of snow, bright water running in rivulets along the side of our narrow road. We know it by the *who-ooo-who* of mourning doves, *Z. macroura* culling early morning light and in our hearts the airing out and sudden recognition of all those days when those who loved us told us so and we could clamber up every damp, dogwooded hill and then some. So when a man makes the promise another has before how can we not recognize each season yet to come.

Sunset from the Window of a Rented Summer House

They skipped, our mothers, down the path to the sea. Through wild phlox, beach plums, prickly clusters of pasture rose. Our mothers were naked. Their backs. Their buttocks—we were shooed from the window. By our fathers, who took matters in hand. It was August. Foghorn, ferry, the forking cry of gulls. Pink froth bibbed the outgoing tide. Life-listers flit across sea-bleached shells. Our fathers were husbands who kissed their wives. We pressed our noses to the glass. We were still too young to see ourselves.

Vitreous Floaters

The eye, like a child, relaxes: ducks in the bath fake ducks on a pond, people wading behind them. In the parking lot behind our town's pink jail my son sees gulls. I see piecework of the sky: spittle, drill bits, a feral net, white sun stunned by things. He learns to point: *bird*, I say, *tall building.* But the jail dissolves, fog napping below the flagpole. The bird recedes, flitting against the breeze, frogged wool hooked by weeds, this exhaustion of the eye, gray whorls floating out of reach and in objection's way.

Gone Missing

Forest cat, barn cat, yowler disappeared among the hills. My brother stayed with me in sorrow for days, calling for the cat *cat cat cat* into wicking trees into fog into remote houses of neighbors who had seen a cat had seen but scratch and piddle. In turn we called and called the more, into wind and branching rain, slicked glass edge of the blue black lake, gray bottomed boat, storm bleached crabs, a circle of ravens circling our voices which circled our doubt, into the scull *cat cat* around the lake around the lake again, the little sluice, mucky stones on shore, wet nettles into the last thin scat of light called *cat*.

In Our Youth Our Hearts Were Touched with Fire

to us who remain behind is left this day of memories

That youth was ours, this was an illusion, but its longing not. We were naked, we were fuel ourselves. Like gods in moonlight we left thin layers of ash in the cave. What we opened opened us. As mimes first learn to walk in place, then into wind, then climb a rope of air, we thought, *Got it*: leaning back, legs braced, we touched a lit torch to our tongues. Live and learn. White gas is not nourishing. One cuts oxygen, sometimes, to live. Communing with gods takes more than a mouth in flame. So we have never done this since. Once air we breathed was fire. This was not illusion: it signals through our life.

Give Us This Day

Quilt back, small duck, dimpling shadowed water. We bring you
bread. We tear our tongues. Turn to our faces under water's soft skin,
brown leaves, white down, our sky as gray as any puddle. My father
cannot keep my son from standing at the edge of order—stones sink,
hands splash. My father who has practiced law—I cannot hold my
father back from tiny things that founder, a child's will, a parent's
word. And so I fall, quilt back, welled breath, folding my father's
arm, my squirreling son, the evening feathered in the sip of wind,
what once was day, bread torn for the prayer which keeps it.

SNOW ON SAGE

Silence in the stillness of snow falling on high desert, sagebrush, the bark of pinyon pine. There is no word for going toward what's left behind. A reference point must be imposed. Hokusai painted snow on plum tree blossoms in snow. He changed his name thirty times. What blurs desert in the stillness of falling becomes the sky's residual edge. As an aged man's hand, finding his woman's, rests like a branch and its plum between her legs.

The Mind Is a Cricket

One wing drawn across another in the feather grass of a distant field, you beckon, a bright silence I can barely hear. Wing *sotto voce* on serrated wing. Courting is loud. Calling is soft. Such weight upon the scapula. Even angels prefer thinking to flight, unwinding the sky from dusk.

SUNRISE IN THE HIGH SIERRAS

Comes by surprise through a glittery xylophonic zipper of sky. We stretch, sit up, shivering, rise. In a ribbon-tying chitter of Cassin's finches. In a puckery frit of chickadees. Lace boots, strap packs. In a krummolz tangle of juniper, grey-green needles of Jeffrey's pines. We walk. On metamorphic crystal-bellied glacial debris. And walk. On wind-belted shadow-warrened surficial veneer. Uphill, uphill, steady up, sweaty hill. Toward accumulating anaglyphic cumulus clouds. The mid-day sky. It's the fourth of July. We picnic, stretch, pack up, and walk. Up the rock scrabbled banks of Fletcher's Creek. Flash rabbled, white water, lilting, our laughter. In dog violet, tiger lily, woodrush, our laughter. Boots off, sweaty socks, in the lung-rousing slick mirror sting of cold water. A sudden gash, sudden whip-kick of light, the rolling crack which follows. *We hold these truths to be self-evident, that*—we, three women exposed in a creek, are up to that.

Watering the Ocean

When Bogart peed stateside of the Santana, your uncle saw the actor in the man. *It's mine*, Bogart said tucking himself back in, *all mine*, casually surveying the horizon. Your uncle said as much about your mother's silence vis-à-vis your real father's name. It takes a story to make up for what a story takes away.

After Kongjian Yu's "Square & Round" at Chaumont-sur-Loire

Who follows *Whom*. & led the way. Toward vertical slats of red bamboo. A mirroring pool of black water. It was Sunday afternoon. The sky was blue. *Who* asks *Whom*. & doesn't answer. In another time I was the sweetness I found everywhere. Square. Sine curve. Line moiré. Balloons rose from the necks of trees. The river was passing by chance. In another time I could fall into the sky and laugh. *Who* turns to *Whom*. & was not myself. In another time there was more than one direction. In another time I could see through a canyon of light.

INTERPRETATION

The wind snaps branches against our house, like cranial bones pressing the brain. This is not romance but the highly articulated squeeze of the body: *Remove me, and earth shall too.* But I have no desire to move away, though wings, pitted just below the collar bones, grow fine-seamed as lettuce in a dream of dirt and high walls. Medical skeletons were once gathered in India. Collected from morgues, accepted from jails, anchored in rivers wrapped in nets, left in sunlight to bleach. This may be why one student fist bumps the ventilated breast, why another pulls back from the vertebrae. Like any woman, facing life closing in, I talk to myself. I cannot talk to angels. Unless, in the kitchen washing lettuce for the evening meal, I listen to the wind, splitting a fish in half, lifting out the spine.

Lullaby

This time the angel was only a white nightgown, wind-shivered and sheer. A road stretched past the angel's hem. Two long rows of trees, roots knuckled and gray, cast shadows ribbed with shadows no vehicle could cross. But the angel didn't need a road which is why we pulled her over ours to button us to sleep.

Sappho Says

She loved her husband on the days he left her beside the well, stones slopped with water, women pressing to fill not their buckets but their hampered lives. Love not those, she could have sighed, who berate you for entering into consort with your heart. So did she love her husband when he stalled against her speaking, her public home? She could have left him but she bore his child, and slept, and woke for time, each breath, the blossoms of her flesh. She taught her daughter how to gather plums before they fell, how to tell the oldest truth, to speak aloud, her own clear voice a windswept branch stunning lovers, rivers, shrouds. I'm sure she meant to tell her that to live within the world would be to live in love, but surely she could not call it love, the day her husband left her in the shadows of the white stone walls, the day they burned her poems and he returned to her with folded dampened cloths to cool her skin, her now encumbered silence.

Talking to Death

Would you have me pretend I am yours? I am yours. Snow falls on the ground. Even horses take as much as they are given. I am, as I mention, your life: when you stand upon mounting mounds of snow, prairie grass rises from its own white roots below. Who among us won't be found resumed by earth? Pretend? I am your voice by my own defended. You tend to the horses. One follows one: you, in the flex of wind. And I? Merely one answer that questions your end.

CONTINGENCY

Adonis was beautiful but aging now, and stiff. The teeth he'd lost to a boar when a teenager he'd replaced with dentures he was loath to leave in a glass. But he couldn't kick with them in, and he wouldn't kiss with them out. His hair he dyed. He wanted to marry his daughter's roommate. He wanted her boyfriend as his own best friend. Each time he thought he'd found the elusive Aphrodite she would turn from his attention and he moved on. He took horse pills for his back. He washed in cold water. He still believed mythology would be the end of history. There would be time again for imperfection.

Every So Often

A dream announces you: the dreamer, plunked on earth without
a shadow of doubt. Even as you look away, history makes a knot.
What once glinted as beaten copper has bleached to the aspect of
bone. And still the body bends in thought. All the editing between
answers, all the doubling back. In a dream what's missing can be
found. It's only probability that earth will kiss your cheek.

Pragmatic Syntax

Was this, like, inevitable, that we'd succumb to *like*? Must yearning
for the world—tree, wet wind, wild plum, scree—finally make
its compromise with distance, the way we climbed above a gorge
to picnic in shadows, on rock. You, like, looked at me, and I, like,
said, *This isn't how it goes in books we've read.* The yearning we
encountered—gave us away instead. Trees burned on burning hills.
A waterfall fell upon itself. The scree of reminiscence wrapped that
hike. But as for us, my love, we did, like, get at least as close as *like*.

Reunion

All the pearls of night, all the eccentrics, wake up next to each other trying to find out where they've been these last long years in the dust born sky. Smitten with life they talk on their backs for hours, marking the stars which fall, swear words, exuberantly flung. Watch how they look time in the eye, each other, themselves, begin to edge over, time turned to terrain, white stones, the earth's buttocks which everyone slides back down.

The Life of Death

He wore white. This was not the new world that comes with trillion part harmonies and gossamer wings, but the world she'd known with the sky moored to the sea by a slash of vertiginous gold. What hovered in the scent of hyacinths, what halyard, what hold? He neither answered nor crossed his arms but welcomed as his own idea her head on his shoulder and paper white shirt while he loosened his thin black tie.

QUANDARY

Who says only an angel can walk across a pond on lily pads? I
did, one sinking by one in the dark, waking—no wings, hands'
weight—pressing against the margin of air. Still, truth was restless,
no thing I could hold. All of us verging on heart failure, tumor,
silencing stroke. All of us herded, dreams swarming, from light.
Dust sediment, seed coats, scrap cargo of sky. To wake without
waving takes discipline. But look where you're going, you waive
where you've been.

DIALECTIC: SAY IT WITH FLOWERS

Has the rose become irrelevant? Ever since we've talked around the phenomena of dirt and scent, thoroughly enthralled with Kant, even thorns are comprehended as elaborations of our thoughts which lead us by eluding us until we call the stinging canticle of self-delusion *self*. If, beyond appearances, we could discern *things in themselves* then we ourselves would be no less by any other name. Yet what but what's unspoken can determine what has fallen, fading petals, to the ground?

THE LUCY SEQUENCE

If I an ordinary nothing were,
As shadow, a light and body must be here

1

Was she walking? Was she waving? After three million years was she willing for attention? It was 1974, the twenty-fourth of November, a Sunday, in the morning. Sometimes it takes that long. A fragment of forearm surfaced from the dusty rock stratum near the Awash River in Ethiopia. A fragment of femur, a pelvis, a fragment of skull. She would have been three and a half feet tall, walking upright with valgus knees and lumbar curve. She was twelve years old when she died. *Australopithecus afarensis.* From the south, from afar. Lucy.

2

In 1974, a student of the body in motion, I lived in a room with unshuttered sash windows. My first true love had chosen someone else. One night, following the arc of a crescent moon, I opened the farthest window which is how Lucy's goat got in, with hollow horns curving backwards, leaping over my bed, which is how I heard a bleating heart, turned to count falling stars, divided lights, scattering beads of fresh fresh-starts, not only to learn the heart was my own, but a goat had put a lamp in my hand, unlike the gods who lead the willing with moonlight, while the unwilling they drag.

3

A lamp in the window you might ignore. But a seeming goat? A surfaced heart? How close the last century, the wind of the one to come. As blood to a body, moisture to stone. Look: shimmering beads of diamond glass. Look again: horns etched among the stars, tail of night lengthening, swatted by wind. Each moment a vigil, her face the face you give your life to see. Will she know you by heart? Will she speak her mind? Let go the beads. Follow the stars. How close can you get to night without being in the dark?

4

Ours was a bed of light, left behind. Hers, a bed of stone. Locus, matrix, stratum. The architecture of a body responds to its environment. Passing from biosphere to lithosphere is anything but random. Minerals, dissolved by minerals, precipitate in pores, molecule displaced by molecule. Yet most bones do not become a fossil. Most fossils won't be found. Insufficiency is central to the soul. Rifted uplift, ruptured cloud—was I looking in the distance for what I had in hand? *Lucy, luminous, lunar, light.* Not every fragment is a bone. No bed is eternal.

5

Another sad death, this one in Sicily. It was 304 AD. That's the extent of the truth. In protest or in celebration, the rest is managed say-so: taking a vow of celibacy, a young woman has a dream: to restore her mother's health, she will give her dowry to the poor. Her suitor has her arrested, the judge orders her from the courtroom to a brothel. But she will not be moved by oxen, nor burned though surrounded by flames. She dies by sword. *Santa Lucia.* In ironic tribute to her name, she is given the shortest day of the year, her bones dispersed as relics to Rome, Naples, Verona, Milan, Germany, Sweden, and France. Her soul is what we tell of it.

6

The setting is not for keeps, the lower Kada Hadar in dimensional motion, sea, stone, stratigraphy asunder. The sun so stretched out its rays are falling off, no horizon for certain, no shadow, no view. No aftermath inevitable, not how each season veins with dust, not how earth will prove a lover's grip, not how to form a pubic arch or public square. Even now, given that we're knocking on a mirror, who will answer? Who can penetrate the dark? Archeology is linear: Lucy in her bones. Anthropology is circular: the story of her bones in ours. Phenomenology is spherical: an episodic metaphor, shadow turning over shadow. Real life isn't geometric.

7

Looking ahead, a year is so long. Looking back, each day lifts from a meadow of wings. These words, these waves in the brain. What if they could cradle us, amplified by certainty? Is it the voice which fails? The lamp in hand? Time, come with me now. I will tell the story. I will tell the end again. White goat of stars, offering presence without proximity. Her genesis is ours. Her bones, our wrested breasts of history. How close they came to staying in the dark. How haunting now, behind glass.

The Only Native Palms
in Western North America

We left the road for water falling, splattering dust to rock to pitted path and the yellow flowers of brittle bush. We pulled off our shoes, planted our feet beneath—fire-knotted, blackened up the bark—the only native palms in western North America. One of us wouldn't cross the stream, another got her trousers wet. We splashed our faces, spoke in all the accents of the world: Cahuilla women, *powerful ones*, are these your songs which scold our own? We learn the road by its exits, heat rising from the pavement, dinosaurs housing gas for cars. We learn *indigenous* by shells. Waking at night we squat on the moon-plowed earth. Shadowed by the saplings of these palms, older women wake beside us, their mouths perfect airholes in the soil, their hands powder on the wings and legs of insects. *We are the wind which hovers*, they sing, each word a wishing well.

Standing Before the Doorkeeper of the House of Amun

If this is where we must go, feet bound, veins drained, dried with salt, resinous rough linen wrapping our flesh in place, does it matter the vows we spoke on granite steps swept—not yesterday. We wore flags of white silk. We danced. We were carried away. Days filled with doors as a palette of dreams: ochre, wrought iron, paprika red. Years later we parted as dead. The marriage brain was taken through the head, each organ placed in its canopic jar. Save for the heart, left in place. In order that, years passed again, we could stand before Osiris, source of life, the heart upon one scale pan of the scales, a feather on the other, to see at last—the past is light! Only then, our vows dissolved as through a veil of muslin thread, could we step across the opening of the mouth to turn toward what, though bright, remains unsaid.

Awakening

All winter under ice bluegills keened lake water with their mouths,
sucking the gray sky close, brown leaves that parented wet sand,
beaches concealed beneath the undersides of cars. When we arrived
the air had thinned. Ice had broken into patches exposing the lake's
dark water. Bluegills were holding their breath. Or so it seemed as
we touched the year's first fruit, small bones laced along the banks.
Our son ran off kicking rocks against the hubcaps of our parked car
saying No. No. No. But that small word could not restrain tin horns
snarled in the dirt. Thin hands flung up from lake bottom. The fish,
not fish at all. We held our son even while he tugged, pointing to the
car. No, he was saying as if we didn't really know.

Reference Point

Where we were did not make us who we are, but who we were once filled a sunlit bathroom: one, half the other's age, seated on a green wooden stool, explaining *things* to which the elder, then so young, listened in the midst of hairspray, the iron hissing steam, and the younger heard her *listening* which changed sentences from chatter to virtual space. They kept talking. Filled the yellow kitchen with *sorting out* and *chiming in*, bluffs called, shrugs teased, gallon wine from the package store. All that talking. All that *mulling over.* Filled summer afternoons on the wide front porch, bare toes in the helix of morning glory tendrils trellised on string until bees, pestered from petals, tried to sting. They had their iffy moments. They had their empty stretches. When the Buddha tapped their shoulders *ahem ahem* they tried to *get a hold of* which led to *out of sight.* Which led to *letting go,* which led to *seeing light.* On the silk-wrapped pistol underneath the mattress of the elder's double bed. On the terror of feeling in the younger's head. All that *calling into question* to *get the gist* filled the empty future with bereavement's genesis.

CLARK'S NUTCRACKER

Cairns. And a granite saddle. Middens and whitebark pines. We are carrying water, warnings, extra socks. *Come little, come little,* lengthen the *creeelk* of you. Bonny gray, black wings, a beak to break and bury clouds of seeds in soil. And on return? That is my dilemma. Such a repertoire of cracks and pitch, such a kibitzing of sound. If in one seed a forest. If in one craw new vows. Winter shills the edge of rock. Summer shucks and cossets storm. Your *won't* exacts what I must do. *Nutrifraga columbiana* perch in the pines they planted. Probe cones, prod scales, pouch seeds, ascend the sky and *kraaa kraaa* scat with creek and wind. The high Sierras strut triangulation's network. Rifted peaks rise from their detritus. While we're talking we are walking among ten thousand unseen views. Rock rubble, cliff crevice, litter of bark and lichen. Another fall can be averted if I do not return for you.

Shakespeare's Genome

Theater takes it out of you. The doubt. The damnation. Our genome puts it back.

We are weathered by each other and by each other worn.

In the audience of leafy trees, so many birds, born to sing. For show. For tell.

For any word encountered, proximity is married to the view.

And love awakens, bound by a script made new.

Descriptive Study

Someone is a window. Someone is an eye of wind. Diane is someone.

An aggregate of one. Who is *she*, wondering who she is? Diane ties her hair back to see through the body's sleeve:

sidewalks, empty window boxes, burning incense, banging doors. Chant and descant, here on earth. Also graph paper, leaf shadows, lab coats, biscuit crumbs.

Diane comes from a long line of windows. In wind, she opens them. They call her into question: *Diane*, French for the Latin *Diana*, from *dyeu* which means *divine*.

Diane is fond of her etymologic cousins: *journey, quotidian, psychedelic*. But not *adieu*. Even in French Diane does not like to say goodbye. *À bientôt*, she says instead. *À la prochaine*.

Diane prefers silence in the morning. A chorus around her heart.

Diane loves standing stones, wind turbines, empty barns, and irony. And when she sees a rainbow, loose at both ends. In rain. In tattered light.

Diane meets Diana in London. They both have red hair. They are seeing the same doctor. They each depart by train from St Pancras. Diana to Peterborough. Diane to Paris.

Diane misses no one until she sees them again. And then. Such waves of longing, tidal and elemental.

Diane leans into wind which is air when air leans back.

Diane was never married to the chase. Her bows are parenthetical. Her arrows, pinions for the sky.

In French, Diane shares the moon with eyeglasses and toilet seats.

And virginity? With no evolutionary advantage it would be saved unnecessarily.

Because, said her mother, you are NOT the center of the universe. Because, said her mirror, you ARE the universe. Diane walks away from where she stands.

An eye cannot see itself. When all is said and done.

Diane has sung in a circle of women. She used to dance. She no longer bakes bread. She dreams she wakes at the source of the Seine. There is always a context.

Diane's heart has a murmur. The cardiologist graphs its syncopation. They both watch blood swill back from where it came.

Diane is grateful for ordinary days. Days that rise to the occasion.

Diane was named for two Annas, one on each side of the family. Her name is not her own.

What's The Matter

> *I know I am a mortal, a creature of a day; but when*
> *I search into the multitudinous revolving spirals of*
> *the stars my feet no longer rest on earth*
>
> CLAUDIUS PTOLEMY

1

What passes through might not be detected. Beneath ponderosa pine, box elder and spruce, beneath sediment, sandstone and mica schist, beneath pegmatitic igneous folds, beneath backfilled miles of shafts and drifts, at the bottom of a gold mine in South Dakota, through a tunnel repurposed with wire mesh, sprayed shotcrete, fluorescent light, shielded by steel and purified water, in a nested titanium xenon-filled vat, we are searching for dark matter. It is the quietest place on earth. The sun can't interfere. Nor radio waves, nor radon, nor cosmic radiation. What passes through might not be intercepted. And yet, by doubt or human wonder, what passes through shall be, to us, connected.

2

Even sitting my father stands his ground. He reaches for handholds he cannot see. The names of his children. The year he was born. He will not look up. He will not take another sip. We place a vase of pink hydrangeas on his breakfast tray, stems cut from the hillside he planted. His fingers work the napkin, by long habit wedging clay, work the sheet on the bed. For pink, he instructs, you add wood ash and lime. For blue, aluminum sulfate. These hours of stillness, beaded with motion. *Can we get out of here?* he pleads. Wedging hope, wedging air. *Get me out of here,* he demands. He will not lock the wheels beneath him. He will not hold on. *Is this the real life?* he asks. He smiles at us. *It feels like an auxiliary life,* he says. His hands have a mind of their own.

3

Down they went, and further down, in the Cage, in the dark, men descended. Did they sing? Did they taste each other's breath? They wore hard hats, head lamps, steel-toed rubber boots. Gold was not their explanation. With jacklegs, with pneumatic drills, they bore holes and blasted bedrock. Barred loose rock from overhead, scaled slabs by sweat. They worked by single beams of light. They wished each other well. Mucking ore, drawing chute, loading skips, tramming cars from winze to shaft. The ore cage belled up with three bells slow, belled back down with two. Drilling, blasting, hauling rock. Drilling and blasting and hauling rock. Shifts blurred, lives merged. Ledges and drifts were extended. The bowels of earth, by men unearthed. One ton for a tongue of gold.

4

He placed our house in bedrock. He placed the doors, the stairs, the site lines, the views. He painted the front door red. He felled trees, moved rocks, dredged swamp for a pond. He planted dogwood, summersweet, native ferns and meadow. He played the flute, the recorder, four-handed Bach sonatas. He played tennis, squash doubles, and sang in the car. He knew the calculus, appellate law, land-use regulations. He learned the allemandes and cloverleafs of English country dance. He tested flux ratios for ceramic glaze, optimum kiln temperatures for firing clays. He read new library books, the *New Yorker*, and the daily *Times*, sketching in the margins. He sketched on yellow legal paper and archival pads, on envelopes, napkins and maps. With pencils. With charcoal. With conté crayons. With Pelikan Graphos flex nib pens. In the evenings. On the weekends. Those were the days.

5

Most of the universe is missing. We call this dark matter. Mother lode of cosmic space, it does not reflect nor give off light, but drags on light which follows: a halo-like suffusing fog. Perhaps left over from the past, perhaps a relic from the future. It could be a subatomic particle merely surmised: a WIMP. An axion. A sterile neutrino. Or wino, photino, chameleon, neutralino. It could be baryonic: a MACHO. A primordial black hole. A brown, or white, dwarf star. It could be a fifth dimension, curled around itself. Or a topologic defect, a crack in space. Whether signature or matrix from the cosmologic start, it keeps equations and galaxies from spinning apart. Let us circle. Let us search. Our minds are circinate as stars. To measure this, our universe, through darkness, lightens ours.

6

We speak in concert with what speaks through us. A field of sunflowers in the sun. A whitewashed church. The sky emerging on its tongue of gold. Each sentence has its wistfulness. Is it wind I long for, or my father and the wind excuse? Ptolemy placed the world in a system of coordinates, each place in relation to another and to the heavens. Longitude, latitude, celestial fact: the lodestar held still. Ptolemy placed north at the top of the map. On a summer afternoon my father walked beside me on the brick front path, bricks he had taught me to level in polymeric sand. He carried his cane. I love you, he said. He touched my face. There's no knowing how I knew this moment would be our last. Three days later I answered the phone. What does *this* say about *that*? I will never find my father in the absence of the man.

7

You forget one thing, numinous, retrieve another, drop a stitch, find pattern: *possibly* is always closer than it seems. Blood slips into crevices thinking would have filled. The brain is both perceiver and perceived. Like wood, *mother*. Like mother, *matter*. Grey matter, white matter, a galaxy of neurons kibitzing space. Getting to the next thought, let us mine the ways: *Name five birds*. Right brain, left brain, corpus callosum. Messengers and gatekeepers, a circuitry of synapses signaling cells. The neurologist says frustration in retrieval means a new path's being made. Through branching dendrites, myelinated axons, chemical transport across synaptic clefts. Pumping ions, generating waste, shifting coalitions of *AND* and *OR* gates. Fired, wired, memory trace. Ego of the universe, mire and mirror. Awareness of awareness of *awareness*, love, and fear. *Name five birds*.

8

At the top of the stairs to my father's third-floor studio, a wood relief sculpture leans against the wall. Four self-portraits carved from ash descend vertically on a six-foot milled ash plank. At eye level, my father's head projects fully, his chin, his cheekbones, his sagging neck. The portrait below projects less, the one below less again, until only mouth, nose, and brow remain visible above the wood's planar surface. My father called this *Submerging Artist*. But climbing the steep stairs, you view these in ascending order: each face emerging more fully than the one below. This is my father in context: coming to be, or ceasing to be. Since I don't know where these are, the origin and destination of being, they could be the same. Still, my father changes as I go up and down the stairs. All those stairs. About stairs, my father said *If I had only known.*

9

Just as self is derivative of mind, mind derivative of brain, so parenting the parent exposes layers of awareness. When I was young my father told me to set my sight on the stars and I might get half way. His own last years he kept falling, and each time got up, and learned to walk again. He said that in a lifetime, a few bad years would be par for the course. The last time he fell was on a pebble-strewn path that hugged the shore at Tod's Point. It was July. The sun was a hazy cymbal. He had walked ahead, refusing my mother's arm, refusing his cane. He reached to break the fall. How close earth is to the quarrying sky. He reached, held air, he let it go. He let the mind that threads the voice, he let that go, let go the hope and was-supposed-to-be, let go the paths, stone walls, let go the trees. The air between my father's hands? Vector of the universe, drift of *we*. He let the darkness fall.

Land's End

Start with the sky, you'll never find it in the same place. But every distance crossed returns you to proximity: eroded cliffs embrace a fractal shore. Waves incorporate the sea. Each harbor's nested with row houses. Gulls caucus from the swale of summer above a lilting color wheel of bathing suits and beach towels. Kestrels comb wind to stillness. You scan these words for meaning, as if *horizon* were a place you could encounter by riffing from one shore.

Wedding

The smaller bodies attract the larger, stated Norman Lockyer observing galaxies of *lesser lights* converging on his retina. He meant *as well*: a falling leaf pulls upon the earth as much as earth impels its fall. In that way, I walked across the whole of northern Spain to leave my destination. Even if we never meet again on the way to where we met, you looked up and that was that. We gave our bodies which once were stars. And so related, let us dance! The answer to a question alters chance.

ANGELS ON THE INTERNET

Nibbling edges, tipping words, wings blurred by the topology of design as bits, as bytes, each swill of information readied for transmission, for the motion of the spheres which moves by disembodied intellect—though they themselves can be in only one place at a time. Naturally they do not marry. They do not reproduce. But rainbow swagged on rainbow they do not go extinct. Each filament of light maps upon ourselves as restless pixel in closest known proximity to originating will, each spin in each direction in effect a task engaged which, completed, ceases to exist. Since each closed gate is open. Each wing flaps left and right. In the midst, on the fly, they signal, stack, spool and switch circuits, gates, jobs, chips. They perish to precipitate. As clouds, that is to say.

Rain falls. Morning comes. Birds rise on a column of air. Shall we walk along the shore, river verging, rock to rock? In silence, shall we talk?

In Any Given Direction

Maps are floaty things. And not. To be exact. We say our coccyx was one time a tail. Our sacrum the bone of resurrection. When a man stands at the edge of the sea, when he walks, the weight of his legs falls upward, each leg in turn rejoining the spine. Waves wave away from his ankles. When a man cranes over a book the text gives way to his finger, his chant to the boy at his side. The boy squirms on his elbows, his kippah crocheted from erosion and promise. It is a map when given, the five books of Moses, no vowels, no *trop*. And a map when given back, five fused vertebrae curved upward from earth. Moses is *Moishe*. My grandfather. My son. We say bread we throw is a *missed-mark* once thrown. We say we're not gone when we say *here I am*.

Notes

page 3 ("De Sequana VSLM"): The source of the Seine, an underground spring near Dijon, was the sanctuary of the Celtic goddess Sequana. Archeological excavation (1963–1967) uncovered hundreds of stone and bronze votive offerings dating from the first century CE.

page 4 ("Visiting Gertrude Stein in Père-Lachaise"): The epigraph and phrase "trees weep" are from Gertrude Stein's *Wars I Have Seen*.

page 11 ("Isis Among Us"): "I am all that was, all that is, and all that will be, and no mortal has ever lifted the veil that covers me."

page 21 ("In Our Youth Our Hearts Were Touched with Fire"): The title and epigraph are from Oliver Wendell Holmes's Memorial Day address, delivered in Keene, New Hampshire, 1884.

page 24 ("The Mind Is a Cricket"): In memory of Marc Beckerman (1952–1991).

page 45 ("The Lucy Sequence"): The epigraph is from John Donne's "A Nocturnal upon Saint Lucy's Day, Being the Shortest Day." The phrase "the gods lead the willing . . . the unwilling they drag" echoes Seneca's "ducunt volentem fata, nolentem trahunt."

page 50 ("Standing Before the Doorkeeper of the House of Amun"): The mummy of Kharushere, excavated by Gaston Maspero in 1885, is on display in the Metropolitan Museum of Art.

page 52 ("Reference Point"): In memory of Jean Riley Mock Binford (1931–2014).

page 59 ("What's The Matter"): In memory of my father, Norman Hoberman (1928–2015). The Homestake Mine in Lead, South Dakota, was the oldest, largest, and deepest gold mine in the western hemisphere until mining operations ended in 2002. It is now home to the Sanford Underground Research Facility.

Acknowledgments

With gratitude to the editors of the following in which these first appeared, sometimes in different form:

Arts & Letters: "The Lucy Sequence"
Cloudbank: "Contingency," "The Life of Death," "Possibly, We"
Epoch: "What's The Matter"
Field: "Set in Motion," "Visiting Gertrude Stein in Père Lachaise"
Offcourse: "Sappho Says"
TriQuarterly: "Flying Colors," "In Any Given Direction"

"Sunset from the Window of a Rented Summer House"
appeared in the anthology *Coming to Age* (Little, Brown, 2020)
"Visiting Gertrude Stein in Père-Lachaise" was reprinted in
Plume.

And with deepest gratitude to Stuart Friebert and Diane Vreuls, to my family and dear friends, and to Peter Brooks, fellow randonneur of heart and *being*.